Rhythmic Rage

Rhythmic Rage

Cries for Our Times

Nycki.C

ISBN: 9798988151609
ISBN: 9898988151616

Cover design by Becky Narron

First Printing, 2023

Printed by
Budding Rose Publication Workshop
Alpena, MI 49707

Nycki.C.wgrp@icloud.com

Preface

I didn't know when I started this project that it was going to be for public consumption. Or that it was going to be a Project. What you are about to read are my reactions to an unfortunate series of calamitous events that began toward the end of 2019. It was then that the Powers that Be, the Muses, the Universe, or whatever you choose to call the forces behind creative endeavors, started dropping lines into my brain (whether I wanted them or not). The news cycle and continued personal and professional struggles I was experiencing at the time fanned the flames.

The thing is, those shiny word crumbs didn't tell me they were going to become poems. I was certain they would become the next hip-hop mix tape sold out of a car trunk in a strip mall parking lot. But my limitations as a rapper snuffed that plan rather quickly. I simply cannot do with my voice the things I hear in my head.

This collection of poems was my way of dealing with the shawarma show of the recent past and commenting on a more distant history. Basically, I just started writing about things that made me Big Mad. After randomly discovering an enclave of poets in my rural hometown (with everything that implies) hosting an open-mic, and befriending them, I found my writerly identity of White Girl Rage Poet. And while some of the pieces contained within read as a love letter or plea to younger generations, it is intended for a mature audience.

I do not apologize if the contents of this book make you uncomfortable but encourage you to ask yourself why that might be. I also hope it compels you to direct action in your community. Rhythmic Rage is meant to be read aloud, performed. And it wouldn't hurt my feelings if I heard you spitting bars on your morning train, the bus, or in a strip mall parking lot.

Dedication

for the next generations

Table of Contents

The Beginning

uhh…Happy Birthday Tom Morello?

Flint's still got poison flowing on tap
Motown's on top with uranium and toxic crap
Added to that unmasked viral attack in the air
but bullies with guns are screaming and stunned
asking "why can't I just cut my hair"
Triggered snowflake bums in the state house with guns
shouting that it just isn't fair...

And the rich keep getting richer
while the poor keep getting sicker
and the black are just game for the blue
They say there's riots in the streets
cause they fear a tool for peace
a plea to leash police
to stop 'em acting like beasts
in our parks, homes, and streets

The prez attacks free press
and tells the white guard "Repress"
the right to protest the mess that he made
Rights to arms make the grade
when rights of assembly degrade
Now we've all just been played
by the fascist upgrade
to the American flag
No justice no peace til the racist disease "qualified immunity"
isn't fair trade for badge, blade, or knee

Rise to your feet for phrase of the day
—full accountability
for your acts or inaction
The house on the hill leads the faction
to maim and to kill
Mass media's distraction for ratings
never abating
Keep hitting refresh for thrill
that keeps the world hating

The schools are shut down
and each DC clown claims
Defunding education, vouchers and privatization
dumbing down a nation
Will save the economy...

And the rich keep getting richer
while the poor keep getting sicker
and the black are just game for the blue
They say there's riots in the streets
cause they fear a tool for peace
a plea to leash police
to stop 'em acting like beasts
in our parks, homes, and streets

Witless protection for fake insurrection
Evolution not revolution
You're the cause of the problem
We the people the solution

Rise up on your feet
Push back against hate
at the hands of the state
A call to arms caused the harm in the first place
You don't feel outrage
When murderers get paid
But a child in a cage
Dying in vain doesn't bother you

Rise up
This is a call to feet
Racist refrains the elitists proclaim
"My life matters too!"

Co-opted your god for a photo op
Text of your prophet used as a prop
Bone spurs or not calling the shots
nation's enlisted in a draft they can't dodge

Natives get restless depressed
Their lands repossessed
by big oil and and big biz
He's convinced that it's his...

And the rich keep getting richer
while the poor keep getting sicker
and the black are just game for the blue
They say there's riots in the streets
cause they fear a tool for peace
a plea to leash police
to stop 'em acting like beasts
in our parks, homes, and streets

Harvard guitarist political artist
speaks for the silent
who've been hit the hardest
Trolls say shut up
He can't be that smart
While Bulls on Parade
march on establishment slaying
Your silence is compliance
We're just getting started
The issue bipartisan
Strange Fruit from the roots of
undead racist garbage

Rise to your feet
Free reign to speak
upon this nation was founded
but it ain't your hate speech
so now you're astounded
that lives that you've actively fought to displace
defended by all under the calls
of grace from all creeds, nations, and races
Are no longer afraid to say to your faces
That this is OUR country and we're outlawing racists[1]

---

[1] Lafayette Square, not January 6

Employment

Dear LEO

Even before job search requirements
Tryin' to secure fair wage work environments
Risks to our health but following scientists

Closin' down investments tryin' to make the rent see
Gotta pay the phone and the 'net fee
So Pure Michigan Talent can Connect me

Ain't out here tryna break a glass ceiling
Sixty apps in and can't even get a meeting
Opportunity might knock but the visits are fleeting
Leavin' my brain and my bank account bleeding

Government cheese to prevent spreading disease
It ain't no longer with me
Tell Labor and Economic Opportunity
Claw it back from the propped up
E-conomy

Knocking every opportunity even the last ditch
Fact finders can't find shit with MiWAM in tech glitch
Thinkin' 'bout sending a plea out to G-Whit
Likely obstruction ain't let her do nothin' to fix it

Taxed to the max to come back retroactive
But the state takes and says wait you can't have it
Administrative failure from Departments of Labor
Paying off their mistakes from poverty's neighbor

A year plus the goin's been rough
But the tough givin' up time's up soon enough
Can't pour jack from a cup with a hole in it
Left high, dry, and hustlin'
Raw dogged by the government

Master's Degree

Look at this liberal arts master's degree
Hung on the wall for all to see
A little battered from bureaucracy
A subtle reminder to be proud of me

They said it taught me to think critically
Told us great jobs were an inevitability
Because businesses surely will value creativity

Behold this luxury priced master's degree
Hidden away for lack of utility
You see it's not science, math, engineering, or technology
But arts, education, and humanities

Use it now to help build back the economy
Start right here in fast food and hospitality…

Diversity Cosplay

I see you dressed up in your diversity cosplay
Pretending what you do matches what your words say
Take the gag order off HR and see how you rate
On the disparity metric in what you pay

Check the difference between what you pay men and women
Line it up now for those with more melanin in 'em
And explain now how a variation in gender and pigment
Doesn't affect the amount that you're spending

Now put it next to the debt that each one incurred
For them to be worth it just to be burdened
With absurd hurtful words from herds of the privileged
"Affirmative action got you hired up in this bitch"

Equal in the eyes of the law says the government
But the legislature can't claim that they're innocent
1964, '73, and '90 came and went but
the beginning was not meant to be the end of it

Legislating your hate through revisionist history
Passing bills about who you think we shouldn't see
If we're paying attention, why isn't a mystery
Average age of those representing us is...63

It comes as no surprise to discerning eyes
Under the guise of the never-ending reprise
That voting fraud lies are designed to screw us
As they continue to block that Act named for John Lewis

Trying to maintain an outdated status quo that
Your voice only counts if you're cis white male rich and hetero
Maintaining rights already granted like Roe
Are among those that we must just let go

Sorry not sorry your costume doesn't convince
That what you hold high are We the People's best interests
Scooby Doo villains dressed up in false pretense
Thinking you can stop these woke meddling kids

Education

Student Loan

Sick as hell tired of being resilient
Smart as well but it ain't about brilliance
Educated demonstrated liberated promise
Campaign trail claimin' they were on this
Head of state inaugurated
Ball drop soon as stage vacated
PhDefunct adjunct living out the car trunk
Default assault result
Sleeping on the asphalt
Ticket to the middle class, ha!
Tossed out on your ass
Ain't no recourse
Limited resource
Incorporated bail out
Too big to fail now
Interest astronomical
Pay back impossible
Make it rain mad cash
On compounded principal
Liberal conservative clash
Wolves reign invincible
Sittin' back relaxed on the dime of impoverished
Dollar signs in their eyes sayin' hey you signed on for this

Diversity Statement

"In the Applicant Documents section of this application, please provide an inclusive excellence statement describing how you would contribute to the development of a diverse and inclusive learning community at Blank State University through your teaching, research, and/or service."

Pardon the intrusion
You seem to harbor the illusion
That equity and inclusion are
Integral to your institution
But chill a tick and listen
Cause your diversity mission
Has been a delusion
And what you call normative
Is merely performative

Asking for statements while your towers and basements
Filled with sexists, asbestos, and racists
In need of abatement not hidden not blatant—but wait
Who—you were the gatemen

How many labeled disabled have an elite seat
At the table in your executive c-suite
How many LGBT see
You wavin' a pride flag just for the retweet

Now you're asking how I will fix
Shit in which you were complicit
Pass a pen
I'll show you just where to stick it

No, I'm not dumb
Not academically impaired
I'll write it down
It ain't that I'm scared
I'll show you mine
When every tenured cisgender white man shows me theirs

Trigger Warning[2]

What they say isn't always what we get
Why haven't we realized that yet
They stand at the podium and express their regret
That we can't change anything for one side suspects

That by altering the terms we serve an agenda
To gut and rescind the second amendment
Well-regulated is the oft-ignored remnant
That turns troubled teens into adult defendants

These aren't just peeves that we like to pet
The stakes are the highest and they can bet
That their empty thoughts and prayers will be met
With disgust and derision when our children are dead

---

[2] Originally published by the Poetics Lab in The Community Chapbook Vol. 2

Why I Don't Certify

Subsistence wage and parent rage
Rats caged, obedience staged
Inflated grades, insane state mandates
Class management blamed
When a child won't behave
But "never my innocent babe"
the unwitting adults claim

Unsafe halls, walls become barriers
to block the well-known terrors of
Dangerous minds wires crossed
Access to firearms at what cost
A child with a side arm Failure
to clock signs of future harm
Oxford strong missed a ticking time bomb

School choice no rational public voice
Vouchers couched in a ploy to
privatize that which youth are
required by the state to enjoy
But no funds marked to employ

(Enough) mental health professionals to deal
With issues inter and cross-sectional
Whole budgets need dissection
To move funds the right direction (down)
To the ground floor to those in the posts who
Know that the kids are who they do this for

Administrative overload
Lesson plans scripted, controlled
Rolled into "development" of what you already know
Respect as expert unbestowed
But you "can't" say no

Judged as less when you can't say yes or confess
Pay ain't the best for the stress you endure
Judged at the door to your
Self or grossly underfunded chore

Of creating thinkers critical
Hypocritical political message
blatant and subliminal
that your expertise and worth

are minimal

Reflect on This

Ban the lit that shows the violence
But not the guns or ones that cause it
Ban the lit that depicts the alphabet mafia
Gotta keep that in the closet
Ban the lit that uses the N word
Like it's something the kids ain't heard
Ban the lit that drops an F bomb
Cause it's not your teen's favorite word
Ban the lit that covers sex ed
Cause child pregnancy isn't a problem
Ban anything that highlights a past other than bright (for the white)
Cause you think that'll resolve it

But before you go into the school board fuming
Take a deep look at what your kids are consuming
The Bible, the news, the raps, and the series
The rock songs, the TikToks, the Tumblrs, your slurs framed as
"queries"

History unlearned we're doomed to repeat it
Books burned and banned won't erase or defeat it
Pick up the book and actually read it
It makes you uncomfortable, that's the point, we concede it
Reflection on why on your part is needed
So fuck your feelings, you may now be seated

Not a Protest

This is not a protest song
People have fits say you protest wrong
Can't kneel can't stand can't raise a fist
Keeping lists of what they don't agree with

Try to sit-in they're throwin' you out
When you can't breathe they cover your mouth
Debating hard fact head clear as clouds
Calling out Sheep! if you dare express doubts

Opinions can't share 'em
You'll outrage the parents
School board meetings overrun by
Ignorant Kens, Kevins, Karens[3]
Protesting that their kids—*Shock. Gasp.*
Exhibit social awareness

---

[3] No human with a K name was harmed in the creation of this poem.

Corporate Colonizer Capitalist Cop

The Norse of the North pushed out of L'Anse aux Meadows
Perhaps by rough climate, more likely native arrows
Aimed at point blank or pointing them toward home
The coastal Northeast had some relative peace
After the demise and departure of Leif and his kin
So we'll travel in time to where Columbus begins

In search of silk, spice, and riches of Indian origin
Finding instead sugar, tobacco, indigenous two-spirits, women,
      and men
In exchange he brought grave illness to them
Not wholesale wipeout, but tribes radically thinned
Many more cut down by the score for refusing to give up or give in
One more tragic start, but not yet the end

The next guests uninvited, purely Puritan
A quick trip to Salem gives a grim view of them
The North not as right as they pretend to have been
If you think there weren't slaves, you'd be, well, mistaken
And the remaining indigenous, what happened to them?
Traded to Barbados for some Sugar Beat (beet) Africans
Their "Good Book" allowed it, so it can't be a sin

Hearts and minds must have changed over time, right?
So we jump ahead to 1889 Paiute
Prophet has visions for a dance of the spirit
The Ghost Dance to bring forth love, peace, and land back to all
      who would hear it
A gathering grew large of tribes to dance or to cheer it
The feds broke a land treaty and sent troops, many who feared it

A Bull no longer seated after things got a bit heated
A shot to the ribs declared him defeated
A mere fortnight on, more than just Wounded Knees
More than a score dead–women and children mostly

It's doesn't stop there with the Bureau of "Indian" Affairs
(Seriously why haven't we changed that name yet?)

We don't even have to change the location
1973 Pine Ridge Reservation
The American Indian Movement to thwart colonial assimilation
To mitigate militia-like Guardians of the Oglala Nation
Banks and Means address media stations to call attention to federal
       failures
To honor treaties with natives they made as invaders

Standing Rock yet Stands but Sacred Stone camps
Forced to disband at the hands of "The Man"
To meet oil barons' demands to tap native lands
Where water is life, the risk is sky high
Sacred sites threatened by evasion, half-truths, and lies
2016 to present, corporate and capital still marginalize

Civic Engagement

The Third of November Twenty-Twenty

Remember remember on the 3rd of November to vote against treason, corruption, and corporate greed.

Remember remember on the 3rd of November that Flint, Michigan worries about poison at the tap and residents still pay the fees.

Remember remember the 3rd of November that Motor City boasts toxic ooze and uranium tainted soil, and million gallons are pumped from the lakes for two hundred bucks a year for record profit by Nestle.

Remember remember on the 3rd of November that EPA rollbacks by the current administration number in the eighties.

Remember remember on the 3rd of November the president throwing paper towels at residents of one of our affiliated territories.

Remember remember on the 3rd of November that the law of the land is in the hands of the man who advocated grabbing women by the pussy.

Remember remember on the 3rd of November that the Secretary of Education holds stake in the student loan industry.

Remember remember on the 3rd of November that in country wide health crisis our leaders injected 1.5 trillion into Wall Street.

Remember remember on the 3rd of November the man in charge of preventing pandemic disease kept a ship of the ill out at sea.

Remember remember on the third of November that to cut costs the guy at the top fired the U.S. pandemic response team.

Remember remember on the third of November...[4]

---

[4] After Milton's In Quintum Novembris

The Revolution

The revolution has been digitized
The revolution has been digitized

The revolution has been digitized
Can't strategize to hide the lies
Can't feign the shock or the surprise
When what comes out your mouth is publicized

The slip of your hate will not be passed by
Can't demonstrate your words were maligned
Can't hide the ties your funding binds
The revolution has been digitized

The revolution has been digitized
The revolution has been digitized

The revolution has been digitized
Can't keep your strings from public eyes
Can't admit you're radicalized
By talking heads trained to marginalize

Generations beyond mine scandalized
Yet hope and change within them rise
Using tools of their time to shine
The revolution has been digitized

The revolution has been digitized
The revolution has been digitized

Out with the Old, In with the Youth

A note: Spider mites typically hide on the bottom sides of leaves, making them hard to spot until there's a true infestation.

It's time for the gerontocracy to step aside
It's not a remark to be marketed as snide
The youth of today can no longer let slide
Appointments to posts for entire lifetimes

When the system's removed from a nation of people
It's time to topple its church and tear down its steeple
It has no place in legislating the needs
Of the wider majority by antique decrees

The church has no place in laws of state or republic
So don't let the ink dry on what it just published
Resist the control of spider mites that spun it
Freedom of religion is equal to freedom from it

The halls of power in addition to Christian
Remain largely controlled by old cis het white men
Failing distinctly at broad representation
Of the will and the way of a vast population

Now is the time to scream and to shout
To peaceably protest and nix all shred of doubt
That people have power to crush dubious clout
To raise hell, drop heaven, and vote them all out

Please Vote

Before speaking truth to power
Ya gotta know who holds it
It's not the ancient souls confident they own it

Not oligarchs in board rooms making choices for you
Not the gen that goes Boom deriding the civil rights movement

Not the lounging billionaire classes shouting "get off your asses"
Not the ivory tower theorists, sans praxis, gatekeeping access

Not the shills on The Hill pushing lobbyist bills
Not the elected with skills but no will to use 'em

Not those who deplore the new that hasn't come before
Not the wolves at the door always insisting on more more more

So I speak now to power though you don't think you hold it
Eighteen and up, make this your moment
Midterm and local, school board to comptroller
Gen Z, Millennials, and some Gen X holdovers
You number enough for a civic makeover

This is the opportunity to not let it pass us
Now off to the polls with our voting booth access

The Pledge of Allegiance, Revised

I pledge allegiance to the soldiers but not the war machine that
      sends them
I pledge allegiance to the ones that rather than wage wars aim to
      end them
I pledge allegiance to the veterans but not to those who fail to
      support 'em when the wars end

I pledge allegiance to the activists and advocates trying to repair
      holes in the country's tapestry
I pledge allegiance to the ones trying to avert international
      catastrophe

I pledge allegiance to the elders who fought for the rights I have
      before I was a twinkling
I pledge allegiance to the agitators hell bent on keeping them from
      shrinking

I pledge allegiance to the indigenous who were here before
      colonizers infiltrated
I pledge allegiance to the immigrants who make the nation great in
      the face of blind hatred

I pledge allegiance to the first amendment that gave me rights to
      write this
I pledge allegiance to the privileges that gave me a voice to fight
      with

I pledge allegiance to justice and truth without caveats
I pledge allegiance to the youth who know material is immaterial
      and the least of what represents us

I pledge allegiance to the equal rights of all, not some
I pledge allegiance to the voting rights of all, not some
I pledge allegiance to accessibility for all, not some
I pledge allegiance to bodily autonomy for all, not some
I pledge allegiance to freedom for all, not some
I pledge allegiance to liberty and justice for all, not some

I pledge allegiance to truth and justice but America has lost its way
I pledge allegiance to those who stand and fight another day

Six Supreme Injustices

Toppling dominos, one two three to blast us back to the past
Four five six fixed in your sights, no need to ask
Writing's on the walls of the hallowed halls of injustice
Impartiality in SCOTUS has quite clearly rusted

Your marble tower's guarded by cold iron gates
Claiming you're enacting the will of people and states
Checks polling—wait, on one's nerves it grates
Partisan decisions from wigged stone-aged pates

Ignoring the truths designed as self-evident
Overturning decades of established precedent
Who is it exactly that y'all think you represent
The will of the people, or the will of the one percent

All people are equal no matter the presentation
Who and how one loves are not up for deliberation
Nor is your take on what constitutes creation
Or what's in one's pants or their prescribed medications
Rights granted by birth don't need enumeration

If we're going to protect the state of our union
The pen is the might of our nation's evolution
Take advice from the framers, draft a new constitution
Here is Line One you can use for the new one
These truths and these rights extend to all humans

The News Cycle

Painting the Racism Red

Cracks in the paint and cracks in the pavements
Painting the racism red doesn't erase it

Cracks in the symbols and cracks in the placements
Painting the homophobia orange is just another debasement

Cracks in the facade and cracks in public statements
Painting the antisemitism yellow shows fear to face and displace it

Cracks in the foundation and cracks in the casements
Painting the hate slate green doesn't change what the phrase meant

Cracks in the sidewalks and cracks in education
Painting the bigotry blue doesn't cure the ailment

Cracks in accountability and cracks in administration
Painting the misogyny indigo blindly changes stations

Cracks in the boards and cracks in the (de)fence
Painting the xenophobia violet only amplifies the silence[5]

---

[5] https://www.thealpenanews.com/news/local-news/2022/05/aps-apologizes-for-glossing-over-hate-speech-on-property/

For Sale: One Nation, Under Fire

Disco lights fade under Starry Colorado skies
Lights no longer shine bright from 21 Texans' eyes
Buffalo's Top market not so Friendly on the East Side
New York City subway not a safe ride
Newport News flash wrath of a child

Again we begin with the New Year Same Lies[6]

How many red flags do we have to raise
Which of "their" loved ones must the next bullet graze
When does the response go beyond the clichés
Who's gonna act while Congress thinks and prays
Why do we still have this conversation every. few. days.

How many times will we hear the same shit
Before legislators pass literally anything to deal with it
What shifty platitude can we expect them to give and

Where can we find their corporate sponsors and lobbyists

---

[6] New Year, Same Lies is after the Poetics Lab's annual New Year open mic
theme

Acknowledgements

Among the countless humans to thank are those who tolerated unsolicited first drafts with grace and diplomacy and responded with love, encouragement, and constructive feedback: my sister Caitlin, who was the first reader of the multitude of drafts of the first poem in this collection; my co-conspirator and eventual illustrator of the forthcoming adult coloring book version of this very book, A. Lorena; my social media savvy sibling Brandy Leigh, who convinced me to put these out into the universe in my own voice; Carol, a woman of wisdom who positively impacted these musings by "just chatting about poetry with a friend"; Bryoney, without whom I would still be jigsawing this collection together, Stephanie, who oozed encouragement like it was her job; Crawford, who got it when asked, "Am I allowed to say this?" and assured me that the finance guys won't catch my mistake; Mitchel Dipzinski and Dominique Witten, co-directors of the Poetics Lab, for a place to play with poems and for pushing me out of my comfort zone (as well as being the first to display and publish my writing); Bex for the cover design, formatting, and answering 9367 questions; and to Prateek, Terence, Lenneman, Siddharth, Ankit, Ruell, and the many others who all kept insisting that I write a book.

Thank you to mom for the rhythm. 1961-2020
Thank you to dad for the art of snark. 1956-2022

About the Author

Nyck.C is an ambivert with a slight aversion to being in the public eye who keeps accidentally ending up on stages. She processes upsetting situations through sarcasm, rhyme, and dark humor. She lives in a small rural community in Northeastern Lower Michigan with two of her multitude of siblings and two very fluffy feline overlords.

www.ingramcontent.com/pod-product-compliance
Lightning Source LLC
LaVergne TN
LVHW011414080426
835511LV00005B/531